Swimming with Dolphins

Written by Angie Belcher
Photographs by Andy and Angie Belcher

Contents

Collins

1. Dreaming of Dolphins

My name is Danielle.
When Mum told me I was going to swim
with dolphins I couldn't stop smiling.
I'd seen dolphins in the water near
my home in New Zealand and I'd
dreamt of swimming with them.

Mum took me to the **marina** where
the dolphin boat was moored.
Cathy, the guide, told me
to get a mask, snorkel and some fins.
She told me to put on a wetsuit.
Then Mum and I walked down the **jetty**
to the boat.

Mask: Helps you to see underwater.

Snorkel: Helps you to breathe underwater.

Wetsuit: Keeps you warm and helps you to float.

Fins: Make you swim faster.

Cathy showed me a list of things I needed to know.

Dolphin Safety List

1. Stay with the guide.

2. Do not try to touch the dolphins.

3. Put your hand up when you want to get out of the water.

Cathy showed me a poster of the types of dolphins we might see.

Then I climbed to the top deck to meet the boat's **skipper**. He showed me how the boat would safely **navigate** out of the harbour and into the ocean.

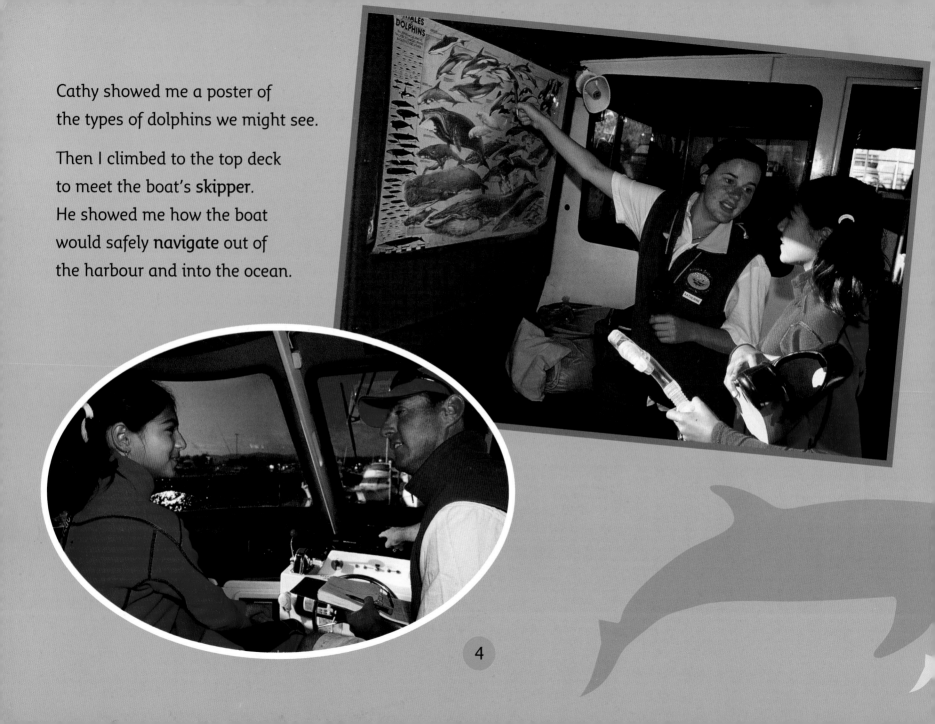

4

We gathered together at the **bow** of the boat.

"Listen," Cathy said. "When we find the dolphins we'll watch them carefully before getting into the water. Dolphins are wild animals. They swim free. We don't want to do anything which will upset or harm them."

5

2. Looking for Dolphins

As the boat moved through the water, we all looked out for dolphins.

"There they are," Cathy shouted. Sea birds were circling in the sky. Something was splashing in the water.

"Dolphins," I called. "They're dolphins!"

As if they had heard me, the dolphins turned and swam towards our boat. They surfed down the **bow waves** and dived alongside us. I could feel a spray of water as they blew air out through their **blowholes**.

The dolphins seemed so close. I called out to one.
It rolled on its side and looked up at me with its big eyes.
The skipper turned off the boat's engine.

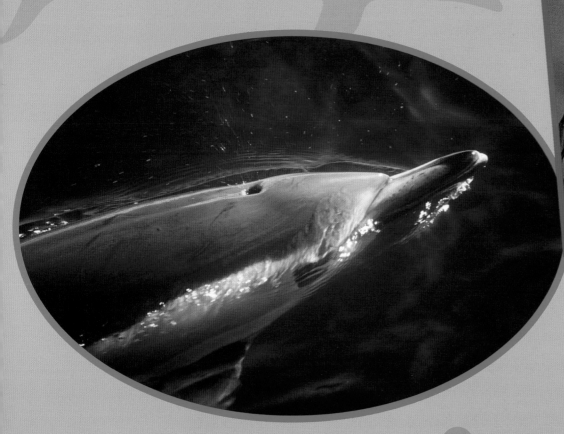

"Climb onto the platform,"
Cathy called. "When I say 'go', get
into the water, swim to the bar
and hold on."

I was starting to feel a bit scared. I wasn't scared of the dolphins ... but I was scared of swimming in the deep water.

"Ready?" Cathy asked.
"Ready," I replied.

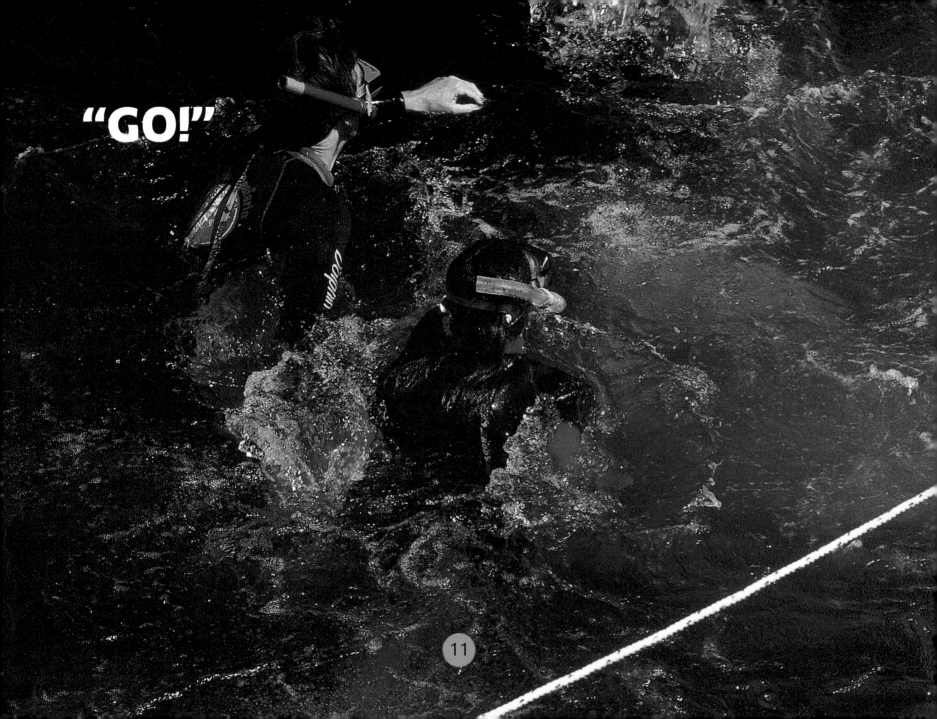

3. Into the Deep Blue Sea

I swam to the bar and held on tight.

I looked down. All I could see was water – deep, deep water. Suddenly I saw a shape. It came closer and closer.

A dolphin sped towards me, then turned and
swam away. Another one followed ... then another.
They were diving and rolling from side to side.
They were squeaking, clicking and calling.
I tried to squeak back through my snorkel.

"These dolphins want to play," Cathy said.
"Do you want to swim with them?"

I nodded my head and let go of the bar.
I was swimming free just like the dolphins.

14

The dolphins swam around me leaping and playing. I dived deep.
But the dolphins dived deeper. I held my breath for as long as I could.

But the dolphins held their breath for longer.

I swam as fast as I could.
But it was not fast enough.
They turned and swam
past me one more
time. Then they
disappeared into the
deep blue sea.

I raised my hand and returned to the boat.
Mum gave me a big hug. My dream had come true.
I had swum with the dolphins.

4. Key Facts

Where do they live?
All over the world, in oceans and seas. Some even live in rivers.

What do they eat?
They are **carnivores**. They hunt in groups to catch fish, squid, shrimps and octopus.

How fast can they swim?
Up to 40 km per hour.

How do they communicate?
Dolphins make whistling and clicking sounds, then wait to see if the sound bounces back off an object. Sometimes they slap their tails or touch each other.

How long do they live?
A male dolphin can live for 25 to 30 years. A female can live for 50 years.

How can we help to protect dolphins?
Look after our seas and oceans. Don't put rubbish in the sea. Stop over-fishing.

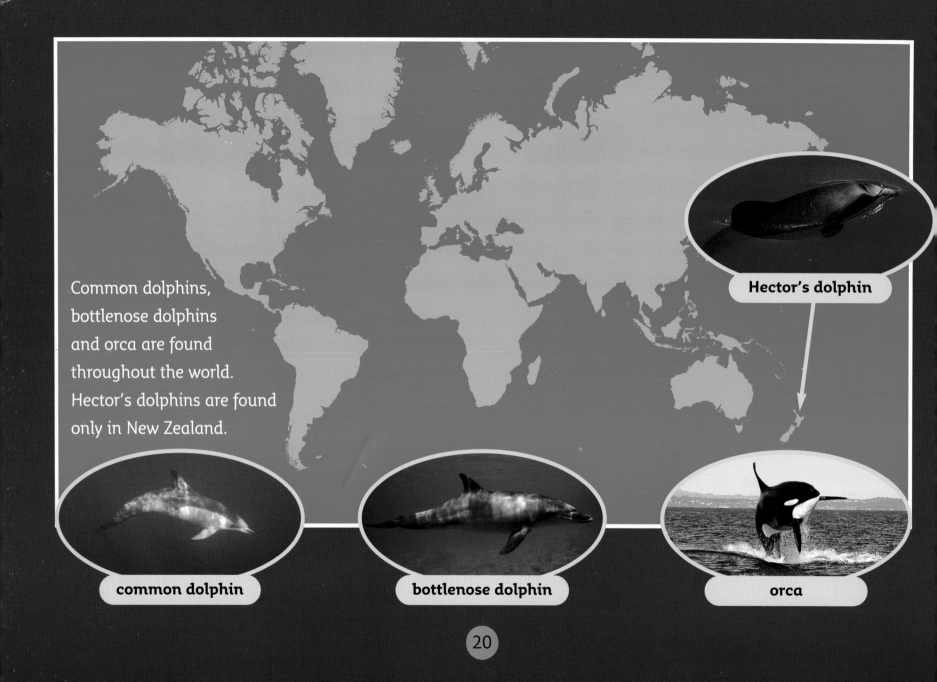

Common dolphins, bottlenose dolphins and orca are found throughout the world. Hector's dolphins are found only in New Zealand.

Hector's dolphin

common dolphin

bottlenose dolphin

orca

5. Glossary

These words are in **bold** print the first time they appear in this book.

bow	the front of a boat
bow waves	the waves made by a boat
blowhole	a dolphin's nostril
carnivore	animals that eat meat
jetty	a place where boats are moored
marina	a specially designed harbour for mooring pleasure boats
navigate	to steer on a particular route
platform	the ledge on the back of a boat
skipper	the captain of a boat

6. Parts of a Dolphin

Tail: moves up and down, not side to side like a fish

Skin: is very smooth. Blubber under the skin keeps dolphins warm

Dorsal fin: used for swimming and diving

Eye: can see above and below the water

Blowhole: used for breathing

Flipper: used for swimming and diving

Ear: has tiny ears behind the eyes

Beak: has many teeth

Ideas for reading

Written by Alison Tyldesley MA PGCE
Education, Childhood and Inclusion Lecturer

Reading objectives:
- predict what might happen on the basis of what has been read so far
- draw on what they already know
- be introduced to non-fiction books that are structured in different ways
- re-read books to build up their fluency and confidence in word reading
- read accurately by blending the sounds in words that contain the graphemes taught so far, especially recognising alternative sounds for graphemes

Spoken language objectives:
- use spoken language to develop understanding through speculating, imagining and exploring ideas
- participate in discussions and role play
- give well-structured descriptions, explanations and narratives for different purposes
- speak audibly and fluently with an increasing command of Standard English
- maintain attention and participate actively in collaborative conversations

Curriculum links: Geography

Interest words: bow, bow waves, blowhole, carnivore, jetty, marina, navigate, platform, skipper

Word count: 812

Resources: small whiteboards and pens

Build a context for reading

This book could be read over two sessions.

- Read the title and blurb with the children and skim-read the contents page. Discuss what the book might be about and ask what kind of text it is. (It is a recount text that retells real events and it contains factual information about dolphins.)

- Walk through the book with the children and discuss the photographs with them.

- This book is about a very exciting event. Ask the children what they would choose for a birthday treat.

- Ask the children how they can make their reading sound exciting. Then model how to read the first pages expressively using different intonation for speech.

Understand and apply reading strategies

- Ask the children to read the book silently and independently up to p18. Then ask each one to read a short section aloud and observe fluency and expression, particularly of direct speech, prompting and praising where appropriate.

- Ask the group to practise expressive reading. How can they show excitement in their voices?

- Find words with the 'ea' spelling pattern. Tell the children that some of these words have the same